IF YOU WERE A KID IN A
Medieval Castle

BY JOSH GREGORY
ILLUSTRATED BY SEBASTIÁN GÓMEZ

CHILDREN'S PRESS®

An Imprint of Scholastic Inc.

Content Consultant
James Marten, PhD, Professor and Chair, History Department, Marquette University, Milwaukee, Wisconsin

NOTE TO THE READER, PARENT, LIBRARIAN, AND TEACHER: This book combines a historical fiction narrative with nonfiction fact boxes. While all the nonfiction fact boxes are historically accurate and true, the fiction comes solely from the imaginations of the author and illustrator.

Photos ©: 9: Philartphace/iStockphoto; 11: Lorena Nasi/123RF; 13: Eduardo Gonzalez Diaz/Dreamstime; 15: Mar Photographics/Alamy Images; 17: ullstein bild - Archiv Gerstenberg/The Granger Collection; 19: Zsolt Szabo/iStockphoto; 21: Sergei Kasakov/Dreamstime; 23: aerogondo/iStockphoto; 25: Odile Noel/Lebrecht Music & Arts/Alamy Images; 27: Dennis Van De Water/Dreamstime.

Library of Congress Cataloging-in-Publication Data

Names: Gregory, Josh, author. | Gómez, Sebastián, illustrator.
Title: If you were a kid in a medieval castle / by Josh Gregory ; illustrated by Sebastián Gómez.
Description: New York, NY : Scholastic Inc., 2017. | Series: If you were a kid | Includes bibliographical references and index.
Identifiers: LCCN 2016038596| ISBN 9780531223857 (library binding) | ISBN 9780531230992 (pbk.)
Subjects: LCSH: Castles–Juvenile literature. | Civilization, Medieval–Juvenile literature.
Classification: LCC GT3550 .G67 2017 | DDC 392.3/6–dc23 LC record available at https://lccn.loc.gov/2016038596

TABLE OF CONTENTS

A Different Way of Life

In European history, the time period from roughly the 5th to the 15th century is known as the medieval era, or the Middle Ages. During this time, the wealthy and powerful members of the **noble** class lived in amazing structures called castles. So did their family members, soldiers, and servants. **Peasant** farmers lived on land nearby. There were a lot of wars during the medieval era. Castles were built to protect the people inside. They often had big stone walls and **moats**. If you lived in a castle, you wouldn't need to leave very often. The castle had everything you needed to survive. Life wasn't always comfortable, but you would be safer and more secure than people living outside the castle.

Turn the page to step inside one of these incredible castles! You will see that life today is a lot different than it was in the past.

Meet Margaret!

Margaret is a servant at Lord Geoffrey's castle. She lives there with her family. Her mother works in the kitchen and her father is a carpenter. Margaret has lived in the castle since she was born. She has recently started working in the kitchen with her mother. She likes her new job, but sometimes she wishes she could go on adventures and see more of the world. . . .

Meet Henry!

Henry is the son of Lord Geoffrey, who has been in charge of the castle for many years. Like Margaret, Henry has lived in the castle his whole life. Lord Geoffrey is a very strict parent. He thinks it is time for his son to grow up and start on the path to becoming a knight. But Henry is rebellious. He would rather have fun with his friend Margaret. . . .

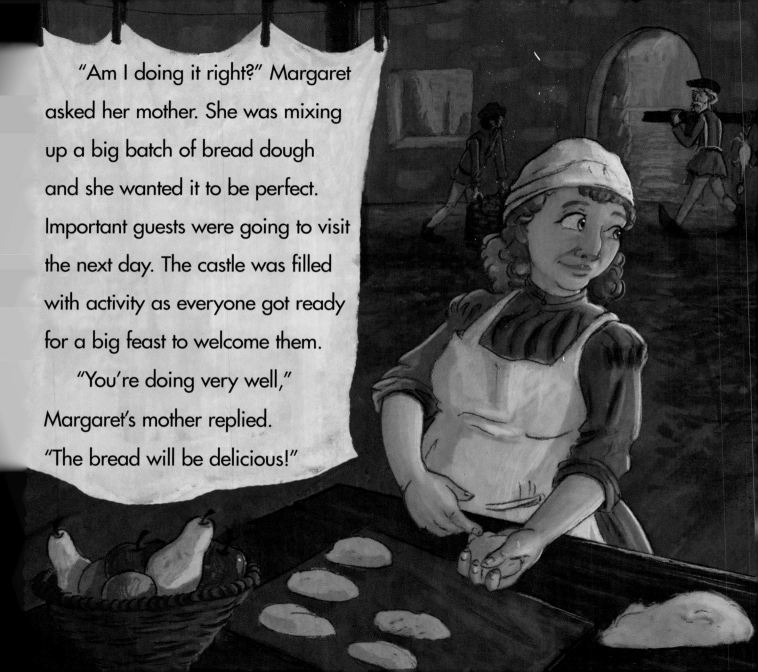

"Am I doing it right?" Margaret asked her mother. She was mixing up a big batch of bread dough and she wanted it to be perfect. Important guests were going to visit the next day. The castle was filled with activity as everyone got ready for a big feast to welcome them.

"You're doing very well," Margaret's mother replied. "The bread will be delicious!"

A DIVIDED WORLD

Medieval society was based on a strict system of classes. The noble ruler of a castle and its surrounding area was called a lord. He and his family lived in the castle along with other people who worked for him. Some were knights and soldiers who helped protect the castle. Others were servants who cooked, made clothing, and crafted useful items. Outside the castle walls, peasants farmed land that was owned by the lord.

Medieval blacksmiths used tools like these to create armor, swords, and other metal objects.

On the castle's upper floor, Henry listened as his father delivered big news. "When Lord Roger leaves after his visit tomorrow, you will go, too," said Lord Geoffrey. "It is time for you to serve as a **page**." Henry couldn't believe what he was hearing. Before he could reply, his father had already left the room.

A KNIGHT'S PATH

Lords often sent their young sons to live with other lords as pages. Pages served their lords and studied subjects such as reading and religion. When they were a little older, they became squires. Squires helped knights with their armor and did other jobs around the castle. They also learned to fight. As adults, they became knights.

Medieval knights wore heavy metal armor to protect themselves in battles.

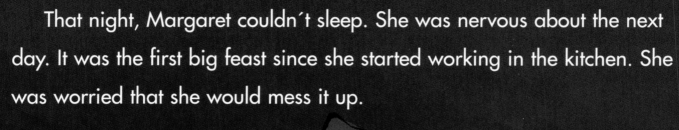

That night, Margaret couldn't sleep. She was nervous about the next day. It was the first big feast since she started working in the kitchen. She was worried that she would mess it up.

Meanwhile, Henry was also having trouble sleeping. He didn't want to leave the castle behind. He wasn't sure he even wanted to be a page, a squire, or a knight.

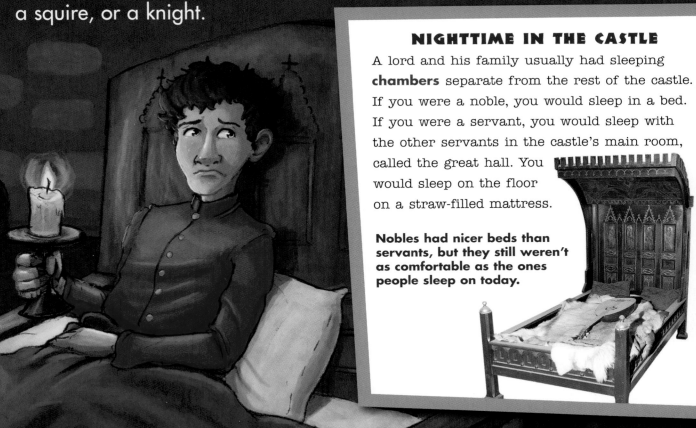

NIGHTTIME IN THE CASTLE

A lord and his family usually had sleeping **chambers** separate from the rest of the castle. If you were a noble, you would sleep in a bed. If you were a servant, you would sleep with the other servants in the castle's main room, called the great hall. You would sleep on the floor on a straw-filled mattress.

Nobles had nicer beds than servants, but they still weren't as comfortable as the ones people sleep on today.

The next morning, everyone was up bright and early. Not long after sunrise, Lord Roger and his knights appeared in the distance. Margaret watched them approach from a castle window. Henry stood with his father near the castle entrance. The men rode horses and wore shiny metal armor. Some of them carried colorful banners. Together they were an impressive sight.

WORK AND PLAY

Servant children in a castle had many jobs to do. But they also had plenty of time to play and explore. If you were a kid in a castle, you might play board games or hide-and-seek with your friends. You might also play with toys such as dolls or knight figures.

A medieval board game

Lord Roger and his men crossed the **drawbridge** and entered the castle. Lord Geoffrey greeted his old friend and welcomed him inside. Henry watched silently from his father's side. Lord Roger frightened him. He looked very strong and he never seemed to smile. How could his father want him to live with someone so scary?

LESSONS FOR TOMORROW

In medieval times, there were many kinds of education. If you were a noble boy, you might learn to read, write, and do math. If you were a girl, you would stay home. You would learn to cook, make clothes, and do other household jobs. Servant children often learned to do the same jobs as their parents. Religious lessons were also very important for medieval children.

Medieval books were written by hand and often had illustrations.

As the guests settled down in the castle's great hall, Henry slipped away. In a nearby hallway, he saw Margaret carrying a sack of flour. "Margaret!" he called out, startling her. "You have to help me!"

Margaret listened as Henry explained that his father wanted to send him away. She agreed to help him find somewhere to hide until Lord Roger was gone.

NO FORKS NEEDED

In medieval times, the biggest meal was served in the middle of the day. If you lived in a castle, you would probably eat a lot of meat. You would use your fingers to eat. Instead of a plate, you would use a piece of bread called a trencher. Wealthy lords could also afford spices, fruit, nuts, and other tasty ingredients. These foods might be brought out to impress guests at a feast.

Roasted meats were popular dishes in medieval times.

The two friends began searching for a good hiding spot. The chambers upstairs would be the first place Lord Geoffrey looked. The kitchen had a lot of good places, but there were too many people there. Where could Henry stay out of sight?

Suddenly, they heard a servant calling Henry's name. His father wanted to see him. "Over here! Quickly!" Margaret said as she climbed out of a nearby window.

DIRT ALL AROUND

Compared to how most people live today, castles were very dirty places. Indoor fireplaces made them smoky. Floors were not kept clean. People went to the bathroom in toilets called garderobes. These emptied into the castle's moat. There was not a lot of clean water, so most people did not bathe often.

Garderobes were made from wood and stone.

Margaret and Henry hid behind a bush in the castle's garden. "That was close!" Henry said.

"Why are you hiding anyway?" Margaret asked. "If I were you, I would be excited to travel far away and see new places."

Henry thought for a moment. Maybe she was right. Just then, they heard a voice behind them. "There you are!"

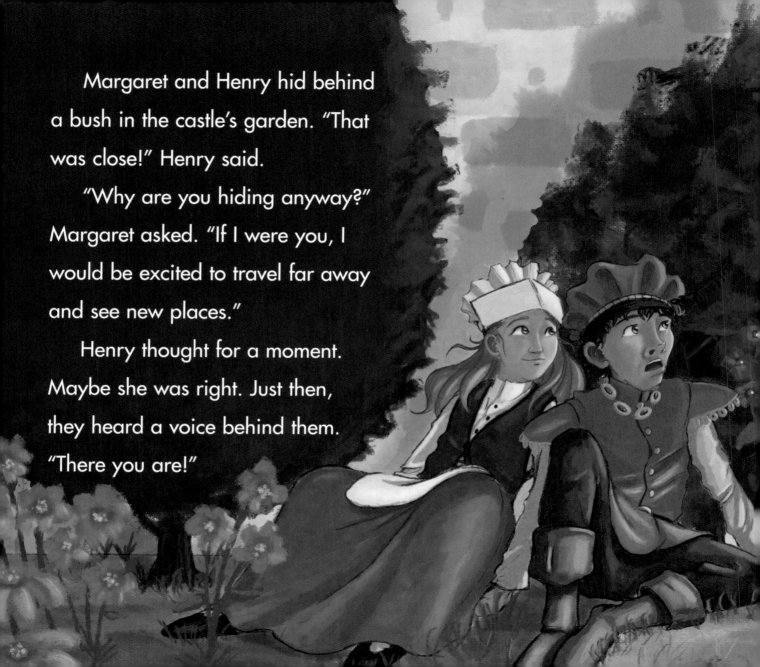

HANDMADE STYLE

In medieval times, all clothing was made by hand. Nobles and other wealthy people wore soft materials such as silk. Most other people wore clothing made from wool. Women used a machine called a spinning wheel to turn sheep or goat hair into yarn. The yarn was used to make cloth. When clothing was worn out or torn, workers called **seamstresses** made repairs so it could be used again.

Nobles sometimes wore clothing with bright colors and detailed patterns.

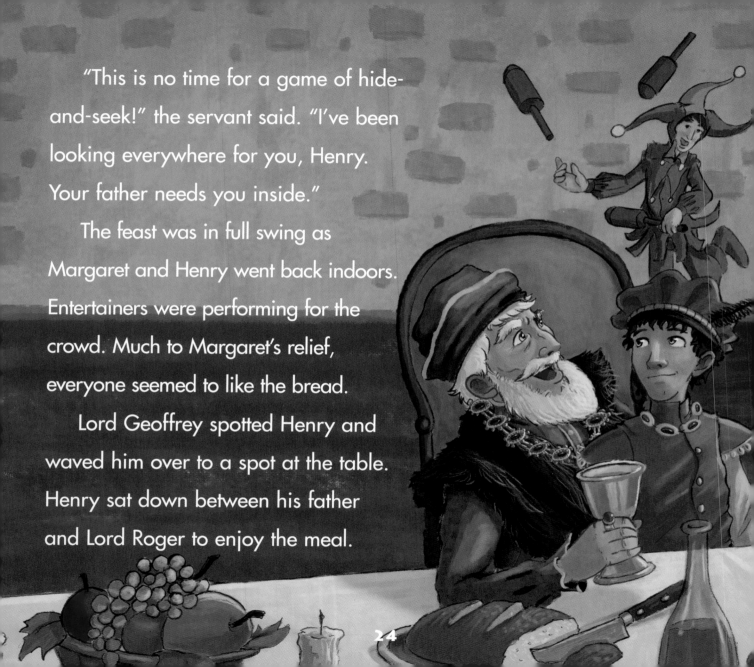

"This is no time for a game of hide-and-seek!" the servant said. "I've been looking everywhere for you, Henry. Your father needs you inside."

The feast was in full swing as Margaret and Henry went back indoors. Entertainers were performing for the crowd. Much to Margaret's relief, everyone seemed to like the bread.

Lord Geoffrey spotted Henry and waved him over to a spot at the table. Henry sat down between his father and Lord Roger to enjoy the meal.

ENTERTAINMENT IN THE GREAT HALL

Entertainers often performed for people in a castle's great hall. If you lived in a castle, you would watch these performances as you ate a meal. Some entertainers juggled or performed acrobatic tricks. Others played music. They sang songs that told exciting stories. Many performers traveled from castle to castle. Others were hired by a lord to live at his castle and perform regularly.

String instruments such as the rebec were popular during the medieval era.

The next morning, Henry mounted his horse. He rode out to meet Lord Roger and his men in front of the castle. Lord Geoffrey was waiting there to wish him goodbye. "I'm proud of you," he said.

"Thank you, father," Henry answered with a smile. Just then, he saw Margaret in a castle window. She was waving.

"Good luck!" she yelled. Henry waved back and turned his horse to begin the journey.

CASTLES TODAY

Most medieval castles have fallen apart or been damaged over time. However, some of them are still standing today. Some have been improved and are still in use. Castles of all kinds are popular tourist attractions. People from around the world go to Europe to see them.

Muiden Castle in the Netherlands is a popular tourist destination.

The Parts of a Castle

Lord's chambers

Great hall

Stable

Drawbridge

Moat

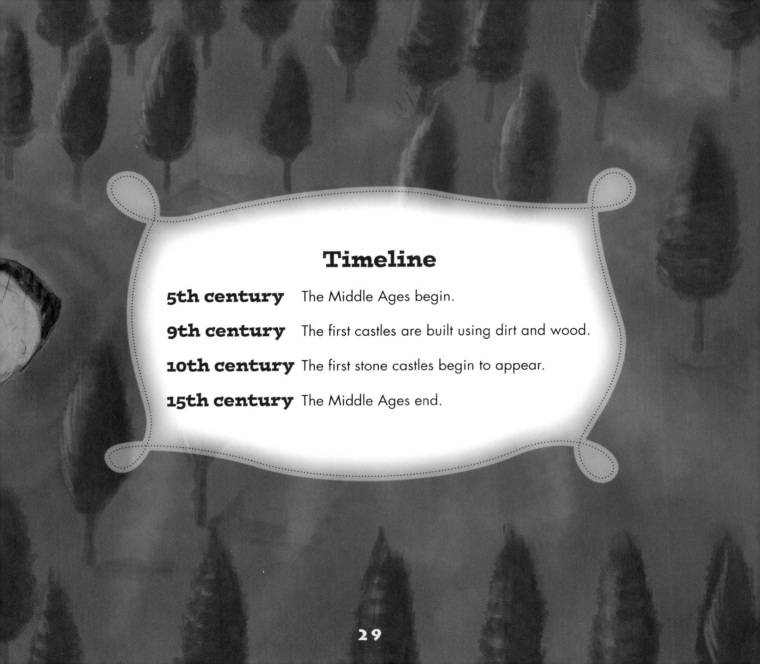

Timeline

5th century The Middle Ages begin.

9th century The first castles are built using dirt and wood.

10th century The first stone castles begin to appear.

15th century The Middle Ages end.

Words to Know

chambers (CHAYM-burz) bedrooms in a castle

drawbridge (DRAW-brij) a bridge that can be raised or moved

moats (MOHTS) deep, wide ditches dug around a castle, fort, or town and filled with water to prevent enemy attacks

noble (NOH-buhl) belonging to a family that is of very high social class

page (PAYJ) a boy servant

peasant (PEZ-uhnt) a person who worked on a farm in medieval times

seamstresses (SEEM-stris-iz) women who sew for a living

Index

ABOUT THE AUTHOR

Josh Gregory is the author of more than 90 books for kids. He has written about everything from animals to technology to history. A graduate of the University of Missouri–Columbia, he currently lives in Portland, Oregon.

Visit this Scholastic Web site for more information about a Medieval Castle:

www.factsfornow.scholastic.com
Enter the keywords **Medieval Castle**

ABOUT THE ILLUSTRATOR

Sebastián Gómez was born in Colombia and immigrated to the United States with his family at the age of 11. There, he pursued his dream of creating art for a living. He makes pictures as a way to bring to life all the fantasies and stories stuck in his head since childhood. When he is not drawing knights and dragons, he can be found playing basketball and other sports.